George Washington Carver
Carver
What Do You See?

By Janet and Geoff Benge
Illustrated by Kennon James

Advance . HOUSTON
PUBLISHING, INC

Permissions
Advance Publishing, Inc.
6950 Fulton St.
Houston, TX 77022

http://www.advancepublishing.com

First printing, 1997
Printed in Singapore

Library of Congress Cataloging-in-Publication Data
Benge, Janet, 1958–
     George Washington Carver, what do you see? / by Janet and Geoff
Benge ; illustrated by Kennon James.
        p.   cm. — (Another great achiever)
     Summary: A brief biography of the African American scientist who overcome tremendous hardship to make unusual and important discoveries in the field of agriculture.
     ISBN 1-57537-102-2 (LB : alk. paper). — ISBN 1-57537-101-4 (HC : alk. paper)
     1. Carver, George Washington, 1864?–1943—Juvenile literature.
2. Afro-American agriculturists—Biography—Juvenile literature.
3. Agriculturists—United States—Biography—Juvenile literature.
[1. Carver, George Washington, 1864?–1943. 2. Afro-Americans—Biography. 3. Agriculturists.] I. Benge, Geoff, 1954–
II. James, Kennon, ill. III. Title. IV. Series.
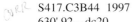 S417.C3B44 1997
630'.92—dc20
     [B]   96-15489
                                                           CIP
                                                            AC

George Washington Carver
What Do You See?

George was born a slave. Of course he didn't know it at the time. And he didn't know he lived near Diamond, Missouri, or that being born in 1864 put him in the middle of the Civil War. He was a baby—just a few weeks old—and all he knew was his mother, Mary, and his big brother, Jim.

Outside the weather had turned cold, but not too cold to ward off a band of raiders. These rough-and-tumble outlaws, called bushwhackers, were in the business of looting, and they had come to Moses Carver's Diamond Grove farm.

These bushwhackers grabbed Mary. She held her baby tight as the men took her away.

After the bushwhackers escaped, they stopped to take a good look at what they had stolen. Mary was strong and healthy and would fetch a good price. But George...what a puny, sick baby. He wasn't worth a penny! So they left him by the roadside and kept on riding with Mary.

Moses Carver, slaveholder of Mary and George, knew that terrible things happened to stolen slaves, and he was very worried. He gave his best horse to a man named Bentley and asked him to find Mary and George and swap them back for the horse. Bentley rode for many miles. He never caught up with Mary, but he did meet a woman who'd been caring for a baby she had found. It was George! Bentley bundled him up, strapped him onto his saddle, and set off through the snow.

It took Bentley seven days to get back to the farm. Moses' wife, Susan, unwrapped the frozen blanket, unsure if George was alive. As she did, he wiggled. So she pulled off his wet clothes and held him close to the fire.

"Aunt" Susan liked babies and children. Unfortunately, her only little girl had died a long time ago. Since she now had no children, and since George and Jim needed a mother, she and Moses decided to raise them as their own.

George was not easy to raise. He didn't seem to know that babies were supposed to drink and grow. He didn't walk until he was three years old, and then only with a lot of huffing and puffing. He coughed so much that he damaged his voice, which made it sound squeaky. It never got better. To make matters worse, he also stuttered, so that people often made fun of him.

When George was nearly two, the Civil War ended and all slaves had to be set free. None of this meant anything to George at the time. He was too little to know he hadn't been free all along.

But as he got older, George found it difficult to understand what "being free" meant. It didn't seem to mean being treated the "same" as white people, that was for sure. He was free to walk eight miles to town, but not free to drink at the water fountain when he got there . . . or to eat at the restaurant. And he was free to go to Sunday school, but not other kinds of schools. The people who made up the rules said that white and black children couldn't be in the same public classroom. The nearest school to George was attended by white children, so George couldn't go.

This frustrated George. Although he was a very small boy, he had a lot of questions stuffed inside him. Questions like: Why did some herbs in Aunt Susan's garden like lots of sun, while others did better in shade? Did those strange little dots on the back of leaves, called fungi, make plants sick? Why were rocks different colors? What made some rocks smooth and others jagged? What was it that made the rose by the window red and the one by the door yellow?

George came up with experiments to answer as many questions as he could. He put some plants in the sun and others in the shade to see which grew the fastest. He climbed sick trees to see if they had strange insects or fungi on them. He mixed dirt from the garden with leaves from certain trees, or with sand from the creek bank to find out which plants grew best in what combinations of soil. He collected rocks and stones wherever he went.

But there were a lot of answers he didn't have. He knew the answers would be in books. But where would he ever find such books, and how would he ever learn to read them?

Finally Aunt Susan saw that George wouldn't be happy with cooking and laundry work for the rest of his life. She dug an old spelling book out of a trunk and gave it to George. Every now and then she would help him along. He looked at the wiggly lines until he saw letters. He looked at the letters until he saw words. And he looked at the words until he saw sentences. Before he knew it, he could read! Every chance he got he read his spelling book until he could recite it by heart.

He knew that there were other words to learn and other books to read. Again, Aunt Susan went to her trunk. This time she pulled out several books. One of them was *Little Women*—the story of four girls whose father had gone off to war.

George read the book many times. Some things in the book reminded him of his life. His father was gone too—he'd been killed in an accident just before George was born. And the girls did lots of ironing and mending, just like he did.

Although George tried to be happy with Aunt Susan's books, they weren't quite what he had in mind. They didn't answer his questions. He dreamed of going to school where there were teachers and books and maps and wall charts.

Even without school, George learned things. He watched people working around the farm and copied them.

The Carvers were thrifty people. That meant they never paid money for something they could make themselves. In fact, the Carvers were *extra* thrifty people. They made just about everything they needed.

He watched Aunt Susan spin wool and flax into thread and then weave it into cloth. And he watched Uncle Moses render pig fat to make candles and soap. He saw how roots were crushed to make medicines and how animal skins were tanned and made into shoes and belts. The Carvers also grew their own fruits and vegetables and raised animals to eat. In fact, the only things they bought were sugar and coffee.

Being thrifty also meant that the Carvers didn't "waste" money on frivolous things. One day George saw a beautiful painting in a neighbor's house and he wanted to try painting. But he knew Aunt Susan would never spend money on paints or canvas.

As he walked home he looked around him. What did he see? Rocks, trees, and dirt. The same things he always saw. But an idea popped into his head. He gathered rocks and leaves and flower petals and berries, then he crushed them together with water to make paints. Instead of canvas, he painted on smooth stones and pieces of wood. And he painted what he knew and loved—flowers and trees.

By the time George was nine, he had become very useful around the farmhouse. He could chop wood and cook, embroider and iron clothes.

Even the neighbors were glad to have George nearby. They called him "the Little Plant Doctor." People came from miles around to ask for help with their sick plants. George would sit beside the plants and study them until he knew how to make them better. Some plants needed more sunlight, some were growing in the wrong kinds of soil, and others had tiny bugs or fungi on them. Whatever the problem, the Little Plant Doctor tried to fix it.

Even Uncle Moses took George's advice when his prize apple tree began to wither. George climbed all over the tree until he found a colony of coddling moths growing in some of the branches. He told Uncle Moses to cut off those branches. Moses did, and the tree recovered.

By the time he was twelve, George had a big argument going on inside him. On the farm he had a happy life with Uncle Moses and Aunt Susan and his brother Jim. There was plenty of food to eat and warm clothes to wear. Still, he had to find answers to his questions. To do that he would have to find a school for black children.

The good news was the Lincoln School for Colored Children had recently opened in Neosho. The bad news was Neosho was eight miles away—too far to walk each day. George knew if he wanted to go to school he'd have to move into town. That would mean saying goodbye to the Carvers and Jim.

It was a tough choice for a twelve year old to make. But deep down, George knew he would never be happy until he learned more. So he said goodbye to everyone and began the long, lonely walk to Neosho. He didn't take much with him—just his rock collection, his tiny wood carvings, and the corn bread Aunt Susan had made him, all wrapped up in a kerchief.

There was one more thing George needed—a last name. Until now he'd just been "George," and his brother had been "Jim." They had been born slaves, and slaves never had last names—they didn't need them. Last names were used to open bank accounts, book hotel rooms, enroll in school, get married, or own property—all things slaves could never do.

But now George was not a slave, and he was going to enroll in school.

He thought how Aunt Susan and Uncle Moses had treated him like a son, and he decided to be known as George *Carver.* As he walked down the road, he promised himself that some day he'd make them proud.

In Neosho, George went to live with a black couple named Andrew and Mariah Watkins. To pay his way he did laundry and other housework. The Watkins' house was right next to the school. This worked out fine, because George could jump the fence at noon and scrub clothes while he ate lunch.

Andrew and Mariah were Christian folk. They took George to church and gave him a special book—a Bible. What he read fascinated him. It told how the earth and the sky and all the animals and plants were part of a giant mosaic God had created. And as he read, he finally began to get answers!

He certainly wasn't getting many answers from Mr. Foster, his teacher. It didn't take long for George to realize he knew more than Mr. Foster. Now from time to time, most children *think* they know more than their teacher, but in George's case it was true. He really did.

George sighed. Nothing was easy. He would have to travel further away to get the answers he wanted. George put the Bible in his kerchief with his rock collection and carvings, said good-bye to the Watkins, and hitched a ride on a wagon headed for Fort Scott, Kansas.

Now thirteen, George found a job as a cook for a white family. Even though he'd never been a cook, in no time at all, he was winning baking competitions. Ladies were even envious of his extra fluffy biscuits and crispy pie crusts! While George was glad that everyone liked his cooking, he never forgot why he had come to Fort Scott.

By fall he had saved enough money to move into his own little cabin and enroll in school—a nearly all-white school.

But this time color didn't matter. And before very long, everyone began to realize that, although George hadn't had much schooling, he was smart—very smart. Students and teachers listened spell-bound as he told them about nature.

Life was happy for the next three years. George spent his summers working to earn money for school.

He dreamed of going to college. But before he could graduate from high school, two terrible things happened, and both things had to do with being black.

As he was walking quietly through town one day, two white men stopped him and asked why he was carrying books. George told them they were his school books. The men laughed and said black people didn't go to school, and George must have stolen the books from a white child. George stood calmly. He had done nothing wrong and he wasn't going to run away. The men punched and kicked George and stole his books. Bloodied, George got up and walked away. Many people had watched, but no one tried to help.

George was sad and scared. Since his books were gone, there was no use returning to school. All his hard work seemed to have been for nothing. The next day George found work with a blacksmith.

Not long after this, a black man accused of hurting a twelve-year-old white girl was hunted down and arrested. As the sun went down, George noticed a crowd gathering outside the jail. Something told him to hide. He crept into the shadows.

Minutes passed. Finally the angry mob stormed the jail and dragged the prisoner from his cell. The crowd cheered. Mothers lifted children up to get a better view. Old men waved their arms and yelled excitedly. The black man begged for his life, but no one listened. George was horrified as he saw the man hung, then roasted over a fire. The crowd went wild. Even the children laughed as they watched him burn.

That night, George couldn't sleep. The images of what he had seen wouldn't go away. He didn't understand the people's hatred, but he knew it was real. Would the mob come for him next? He wasn't going to wait to find out. In the middle of the night, he fled.

For the next few years, George wandered around the West. He went to school where he could, and left when he ran out of money or felt unsafe. He also taught himself many things. He studied strange grasses in Colorado. He crushed and mixed paints from the wonderful array of brilliantly colored clays in New Mexico and painted pictures of everything he saw. He collected rocks in Kansas. To stop his lonely thoughts, he would read his Bible and go for walks before dawn.

Sometimes he got letters from friends he'd made along the way. Once, his mail went to the wrong address—to another George Carver living in the same Kansas town. That's when George started using "W" as a middle initial. At first, the "W" didn't stand for anything, but when a friend asked him if it stood for *Washington*, George said, "Yes. Why not!"

Now, as he went from job to job and school to school, he would be known as George *Washington* Carver.

One letter he got brought bad news. His brother Jim had died of small pox. George felt very alone. He'd never seen his father, couldn't remember his mother, had no idea who his grandparents or aunts and uncles were, and now his only brother was dead. George cried for a long time.

Still, he didn't give up. When he was twenty-one years old, he finally graduated from high school. Now he was ready for college. He applied to Highland College in Kansas. At last he got a reply. Yes, his grades were good enough—he'd been accepted!

George kept unfolding the acceptance letter, reading it over and over again as the train took him closer to his dream—a college education. He could barely contain his excitement as he bounded up the steps of the red brick college building. George Washington Carver had made it!

George asked to see the principal. A long time passed. Finally the principal came out of his office. George reached out to shake hands. "George Carver, Sir," he introduced himself. "I've come to enroll."

The principal did not shake George's hand. "You didn't tell me you were a Negro," he said coldly. "This college does not accept Negroes."

George felt that familiar feeling in his stomach. There was nothing more to say. He walked away feeling very sad. What was the use of working so hard to get to college? It seemed there was no place to go, no way for a black person to get an education.

This time George Carver almost gave up on his dream. In the next five years he tried many different things. He even tried farming, but there was a hole inside of him that farming couldn't fill.

Slowly, Carver let himself dream again. Friends he'd met at church convinced him to apply to Simpson College in Iowa. He applied and was accepted—color and all. He was twenty-six years old, but he'd finally made it!

How wonderful Simpson College was. Everywhere there were things to learn, books to read, and knowledgeable people with whom he could speak. Carver didn't waste a second. He started a laundry to pay his way. Between classes he would rush home to scrub clothes, just like he'd done fourteen years before in Neosho. Best of all were his art classes with Miss Budd. He often brought leaves and mosses to class that he had gathered on his pre-dawn walks. And he was happiest when he was studying and painting them.

One day, he painted something that would change his life. He painted a picture of a plant experiment he was doing. Miss Budd took the painting and didn't return it for a long time. Carver began to wonder if something was wrong. When Miss Budd finally returned it, she asked Carver some serious questions. Had *he* thought up the experiment? Was he very interested in plants? What did he want to do with his life?

Miss Budd explained to Carver how she had shown the painting to her father. He was Professor of Horticulture at the Iowa Agricultural College, in Ames, about fifty miles away. He had studied the painting and thought the experiment was very clever. He wanted Carver to come and study horticulture with him.

Carver was shocked! What about his art? Did Miss Budd want him to quit? He loved painting nature more than anything in the world. He couldn't see himself giving it up, but he did agree to think about it ... and pray about it.

After several days, his feelings had changed. It seemed that going to Ames *was* the right thing to do. Carver saw he could do so much for poor farmers by showing them how to grow stronger plants and teaching them how to feed their soil.

Carver liked the new college. There were more books to read, and Professor Budd was doing exciting plant research. As usual, Carver didn't quite fit in. This time it was because the college had rules about blacks and whites eating together. Carver had to eat in the basement with the hired field workers. Not that Carver minded eating with these people, he just didn't understand why the color of his skin made such a difference. To him, God had made different colored people, just like he had made different colored flowers—all different, all special.

Carver wrote to a friend for advice—Mrs. Liston. As soon as she received the letter, Mrs. Liston boarded a train headed for Ames.

Mrs. Liston was a very determined woman, and by the time she got off the train, she had a plan. She spent a wonderful day with Carver, admiring the greenhouses and touring the grounds.

When dinnertime came, she told Carver she would eat wherever he ate. So downstairs they went with the gardener, the cook, and the other black staff. When news of this reached the Dean, he was horrified. Surely Mrs. Liston belonged upstairs with the other white people! When they told her this, Mrs. Liston replied that wherever they thought was good enough for Carver to eat, was surely good enough for her! The next morning there was a place for Carver in the upstairs dining room, and nothing more was ever said. Mrs. Liston had won her victory.

Soon everyone wanted to be Carver's friend. He had so many interesting stories to tell. The other students and staff could see that he didn't have much money, so at Christmas they "kidnapped" him and took him into town where they bought him a new outfit—hat, shoes, and suit. They also surprised him by entering four of his paintings in the State Exhibit. And they bought him a train ticket to Cedar Rapids, where the exhibit was being held. Carver surprised them by winning prizes for all four of his paintings. One painting was even selected to go to the World Exhibit in Chicago, where it received honorable mention.

Carver liked having lots of friends. One of his friends was six-year-old Henry Wallace. Henry would often get up before dawn to go walking with Carver. Best of all, they liked the swamp. The two of them would crouch down, fascinated by the trek of a beetle; or they would search under fallen trees looking for new fungi for Carver's collection. (He had collected more than twenty thousand species of them.) Henry asked questions about everything. It made Carver smile, reminding him of himself, when *he* was a boy.

When Carver finished college, he was so popular and respected as a scientist that he was asked to stay and teach. He was very excited about it. But before very long, a letter came from a famous black man, Booker T. Washington. Washington had started a school in Alabama called the Tuskegee Normal and Industrial Institute. His plan was to train young black men and women in the South so they could get good jobs and help themselves out of poverty. He wanted Carver to head the new Agricultural Department at Tuskegee.

"I cannot offer you money, position, or fame," the letter read. "The first two you have. The last, from the place you now occupy, you no doubt will achieve. I offer you in their place work—hard work—the task of bringing a people from degradation, poverty, and waste to full manhood."

It seemed to Carver that he was always leaving just when he was the happiest. But Booker T. Washington needed him, and again, he felt this was the next step God had for him.

At his farewell party, Carver was given a fine microscope. He was very grateful; it was the grandest thing he owned. When he got to Tuskegee, he was even more grateful. The only piece of equipment in his new department was his microscope. There were no test tubes, Bunsen burners, or specimen jars!

At first Carver was shocked, but he remembered about being thrifty. He told the thirteen students enrolled in the new department to collect all the junk they could find.

They piled the junk on the floor. Carver looked at it. His students wondered what he saw. Then he went to work.

Pans with holes punched in the bottom became strainers. Bottles with their necks cut off became test tubes, and broken lamps were turned into Bunsen burners. What was junk to the students, Carver had seen as science equipment.

Those students never again looked at "junk" the same way. They nick-named Carver the "Wizard of Tuskegee" because he could make something from nothing.

About this time, one last part was added to Carver's name. Black people were not allowed to call each other "Mr. or Mrs." around white people. But out of respect the students at Tuskegee wouldn't call their new teacher "George," or "Carver." It just didn't seem right. So they called him *Doctor* Carver, since there were no rules against that.

Word soon got around that *Doctor* Carver's classes were interesting. This was a good thing because in the beginning hardly anyone wanted to study farming. Black people had been slaves a long, long time, and as slaves, they did farm work—planting and weeding and picking cotton. They sure didn't want to do that type of work now that they were free. To them, being free meant being bankers, or teachers, or big landowners. Carver knew that one day African-Americans would become *all* those things and more; but for now, many of them were starving because they didn't know how to farm the land on which they lived. The only farming they knew was *cotton*—their masters had provided the food.

Carver wanted to share everything he knew with his students. He began a weekly Bible study where he taught students about character and integrity. Of course, he also taught them about agriculture: how to feed the land, grow strong crops, and keep away pests. He also wrote many helpful booklets. But something worried him. The people who needed help the most, poor farmers—both black and white, hadn't been to school and couldn't read. He needed another way to reach them.

Finally, Carver found the answer. If poor farmers couldn't come to school, he would bring the school to them.

Carver designed a special wagon, and in his spare time and during vacations, he'd set out with some of his best students to show farmers better ways to farm.

Many farmers thought their land was worn out and useless because so many crops of cotton had been grown on it. But Carver had seen something few others back then had seen.

He saw that nature is a circle. When you take something out of the soil, you have to find a way to put it back. Growing cotton had taken lots of nitrogen out of the soil, and that was why nothing much would grow there anymore. Carver knew some plants, like peanut plants, put nitrogen back into the soil.

So everywhere he went, Carver urged poor farmers to grow peanuts, but they wouldn't listen to him. That is, until a beetle called the "boll weevil" came along. The boll weevil began eating the cotton crop. Farmers quickly changed their minds about peanuts. Soon thousands of acres of peanuts were growing.

The good news was that the peanut crop was enormous. The bad news was that no one wanted to buy them. "What can you do with peanuts?" people asked. Farmers soon had peanuts stored everywhere—in barns, sheds, spare rooms, and attics. After a while, farmers didn't even bother to harvest the peanuts. And they were angry at Carver. What was he going to do about it?

Early one morning as Carver was walking and praying, the problem began to be solved. Later, when he was a famous speaker, Carver would tell how it happened.

"'Oh, Mr. Creator, why did You make this universe?' I cried. And the Creator answered me, 'You want to know too much for that little mind of yours,' He said. 'Ask something more your size.' So I said, 'Dear Mr. Creator, tell me what man was made for?' Again He spoke to me, and He said, 'Little man you are still asking more than you can handle. Cut down the extent of your request and improve the intent.' And then I asked my last question. 'Mr. Creator, why did you make the peanut?' 'That's better!' the Lord said, and He gave me a handful of peanuts and went with me back to the laboratory and, together, we got down to work."

Carver had seen the answer. Wasn't the peanut made up of many parts—oils, gums, resins, sugars, starches, and more? What if he took it apart and put it back together in a different way—like he used to take old sweaters apart and knit them into socks or scarves for himself and Jim?

Carver knew that there were three things he could do with the parts of a peanut. He could put the parts back together in different combinations, a little more of one part and a little less of another. He could heat or cool the parts. Or he could use pressure to squeeze the parts closer together.

He began to experiment, and his experiments began to work!

Carver worked faster and faster. He didn't sleep, and when he was hungry he ate peanuts. Soon he'd made margarine and soap, cooking oil and peanut butter, ink and shoe polish, shaving cream and flour, all from the peanut! Next he looked at peanut shells. He found ways to turn them into paper, fire wood, paving bricks, and building blocks!

Three days later, Carver opened his lab door again. He invited people in to see the many jars, bottles, and boxes filled with things that could be made from peanuts. Carver was delighted. Now, no matter how many peanuts were harvested, there were uses for them all. And not only that, but without even knowing it, Carver had started a new branch of science called synthetics.

Suddenly, Carver was famous. He addressed a powerful congressional committee and amazed them with his wit and wisdom. Thomas Edison, the famous inventor, reportedly offered to pay Carver $200,000 to come work for him.

Henry Ford, the man who mass-produced motorcars, became Carver's lifelong friend. The Prince of Wales and the Crown Prince of Sweden came to visit. For hours they watched him work, hoping to see nature through his eyes. Even the Russian Government asked for help with their agriculture.

But Carver believed that God wanted him at Tuskegee, and offers of money couldn't sway him—he was interested in helping others. In fact, in the forty-seven years he spent working at Tuskegee, he never took a pay raise. And he never moved out of the student dormitory, either.

Visitors could barely squeeze into his room, which overflowed with plant cuttings, fossils, insects, stuffed snakes, potted plants, and hundreds of rocks.

When people asked him why he had never married, he always replied that there wasn't enough time. And he might have been right!

Carver was always making friends and writing to people. He wrote to poor farmers about how to improve their soil. He corresponded with Ghandi, the leader of India, about good nutrition. He wrote about race relations to his friend Henry Wallace, who wasn't little anymore. Henry was now the vice president of the United States. Carver got about 150 letters a day, and he answered them all himself!

In his letters, he often included thoughts from his Bible—the same Bible Mariah Watkins had given him when he started school all those years ago in Neosho. Carver had read it every day since then, and still found it filled with fascinating answers to his questions.

Carver never stopped experimenting, or letter writing, right up until he died in 1943. He was seventy-nine years old.

After the funeral, hundreds of people filed through his laboratory. They saw the test tubes made from bottles, the strainers made from old tin cans, the 300 things Carver had made from peanuts, and the 150 weeds he had used for medicines.

Plants and weeds, pots and pans—most people see such things as . . . *ordinary*, but Carver never did. To him, nothing was ordinary. He was convinced that God placed everything and every person on earth for a useful purpose and that if people look hard enough, they can discover that purpose.

And that's what he had spent his life doing—looking at and seeing things others overlooked.

Authors' Notes

5   There is some question as to the year George Carver was born. Most people believe it was in 1864.

8   By the time Carver reached college, he had stopped most of his stuttering, but his voice remained high-pitched and squeaky.

31   Carver wore the suit he was given in college for the rest of his life.

32   Henry Wallace, Carver's young friend, went on to become secretary of agriculture under President Franklin D. Roosevelt and then vice president of the United States. After Roosevelt's death, Wallace became the secretary of commerce under President Harry Truman.

33   The Tuskegee Normal and Industrial Institute was started in 1881. The Agricultural Department was not started until Carver arrived in 1896.

43   In 1921 Carver testified before the Ways and Means Committee. He urged the government to put tariffs on foreign peanuts to give American growers the opportunity to develop their own markets. Carver was given ten minutes to speak, but he so fascinated the congressmen that he was allowed as much time as he needed to explain all the things for which the peanut could be used.

43   Henry Ford and Carver became life-long friends. They made it a point to get together every year. As Carver got older, Henry Ford had a personal elevator installed for Carver to get to the second floor.

46   Carver remained a devoted Christian all his life. He started a popular Bible Study group at Tuskegee, which he oversaw for forty-seven years.

47   Two years before he died, Carver helped set up his own museum in the old laundry room at Tuskegee. It is still there today.

47   After his death in Tuskegee on January 5, 1943, Carver's birthplace near Diamond, Missouri was dedicated as a national monument. In 1946, Congress named January fifth "George Washington Carver Day."